DATE DUE

OC 9 97		
JY 16 02		

DEMCO 38-296

Baby Hands & Baby Feet

Poems and Drawings from the Nursery

Nancy J. Kennedy
David Pegher

1304 Southpoint Blvd., Suite 280
Petaluma, CA 94954-6859
(707) 762-2646

Publisher: Charles Rait, RN, PNC, MSEd
Managing Editor: Suzanne G. Rait, RN
Editorial Coordinator: Tabitha Parker

Book design and composition by:
Marsha Godfrey Graphics

Printing by: O'Dell Printing Co., Inc.

LIBRARY OF CONGRESS CATALOGING-IN-PUBLICATION DATA
Kennedy, Nancy J. (Nancy Jean), 1952–
Baby hands & baby feet : poems and drawings from the nursery / Nancy J. Kennedy ; [illustrator], David Pegher.
        p.   cm.
    ISBN 0-9622975-7-7 (pbk.)
    1. Infants (Newborn)—Hospital care—Poetry.   2. Infants (Premature)—Hospital care—Poetry.   3. Neonatal intensive care—Poetry.   I. Title.
PS3561.E42684B3   1995
811'.54—dc20   95-13814
                                                                                                          CIP

ISBN: 0-9622975-7-7   Library of Congress catalog number 95-13814

ii

Contents

Preface

This is an invitation to an experience... not an introduction to a text.

Accept this invitation without reservation and you will be irresistibly drawn into the poignant drama of newborn intensive care. It will be difficult to stand as a dispassionate witness to this drama. You will be compelled to participate actively in the lives of children who are small and frail in physical stature only.

The poet and artist, Nancy and David, have no clever gimmicks to lure you into this experience. You will not be distracted by their passionate and skillful use of words and pictures. They are humble and deeply caring people with an extraordinary talent to take you where they have been. You will have much to thank them for at the end of this journey— but you will be wholly unaware of their presence in the course of the journey. And that is as it should be.

In contemporary American life, we have grown enamored of technology and its apparent promise to deliver us from toil and suffering. This has been especially evident in the care of critically ill newborns. Indeed, the miracle of their survival has been attributed to our technical wizardry and prowess.

But this is a mistaken attribution and Nancy and David lift the veil on medical technology. They bring us—immediately and intimately—face to face with the hope and despair, the pleasure and pain of life in an intensive care unit. In doing so, they reveal to us the true source of healing—the relationships between children with enormous courage and wisdom, their parents (including those who are yet children themselves), their grandparents, their siblings, their nurses and therapists, and their doctors.

Only poetry and art could take us to this place of healing.

It has been said that a community's compassion and morality may be judged by the way children are depicted in its art. I am hopeful that Nancy and David will be viewed as having set a standard for the most meaningful, caring, representation of children. Take a deep breath. Read these poems aloud, touch the faces of these children, and stare deeply into their eyes, and you, too, will share this hope.

This is an invitation to an experience; a profoundly moving and healing human experience.

Ronald David, MD
Cambridge, Massachusetts

Dedication

This book
is dedicated with respect, admiration,
and affection to the staff, past and present,
of Transitional Infant Care,
The Children's Home of Pittsburgh.

Acknowledgements

We would like to thank the many wonderful people whose support made this book possible:

Harry S. Cohen, Esquire, for legal counsel;

Ron David, MD, teacher, neonatologist, and poet, for his enthusiastic encouragement;

Pris Ebert, Parent Care Inc. for her support and encouragement;

Merle Markowitz, Markowitz and Haas Printing, for his artistry and his generosity;

Peter Oresick, University of Pittsburgh Press, for his expert consultation;

Chuck Rait, NICU INK, for believing in this project;

Sandy Ransom, The Children's Home of Pittsburgh, for the patience and perfection with which she typed and retyped this manuscript.

We would also like to thank Evelyn Jackson, Bryan Rogers, Roberta Levine, Joe Mannino, Fred deGroot, Julie Hladio, Margaret Paradise, Valerie Gass, Conchitta Harshaw, Paul Kennedy, and Kathy Sluga. Finally, we are grateful to the NICU caregivers, infants, and families who have provided both of us with many moments of insight and inspiration.

Nancy Kennedy and Dave Pegher

ix

2

First Visit

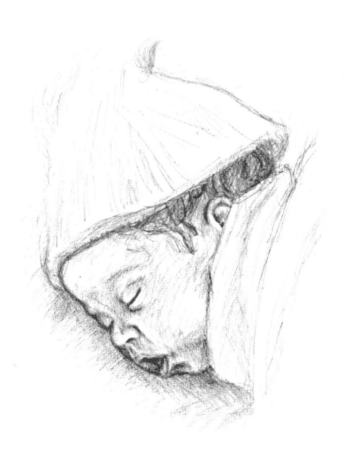

This first time father
had no time for phone calls
or cigars.

He thought he might faint
as he finally looked upon
his first born son,
a shining pink frog almost
too small to fathom.

He held on, studying the baby
and finally found his voice.
"Look", he said, "He has my knees."

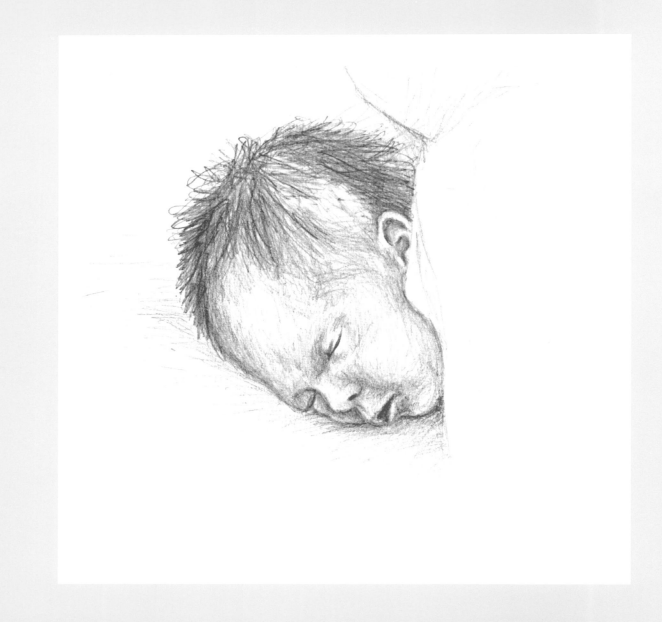

Territory

A tiny gold cherub
pinned to cardboard
hangs beside a crayon drawing
of squiggles and squares.
A medal, a special blanket,
a child's art work,
family photos —
this one is ours.

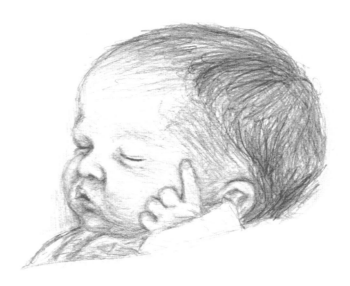

5

Lap of Luxury

Nested in her strong arms the baby relaxes
seeming to sense that he has found
rare comfort and shelter there.
His cry is silenced when she speaks to him
her voice a gentle song meant only for him;
he gazes at her, enraptured by her face
radiating kindness and light.

When Helen holds a baby
her tender wisdom will bless that baby
for a lifetime;
no matter where he goes or what his life holds,
for a moment, he had Helen in his life
and he knew pure love.

8

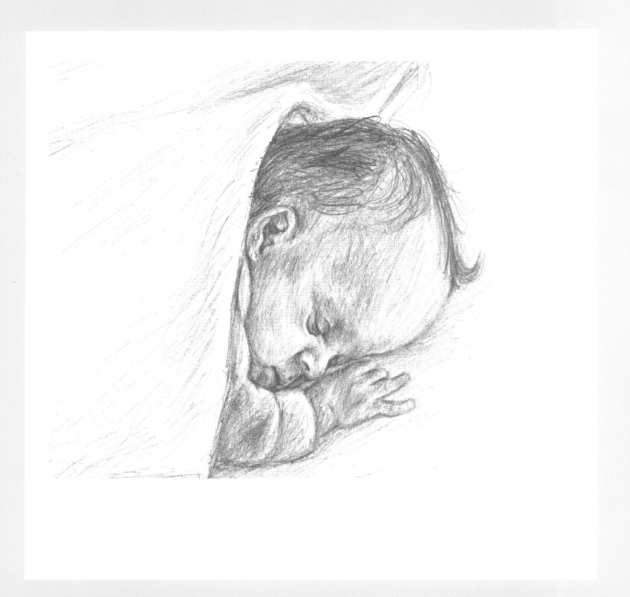

Isolette®/Isolate

My fingers, splayed on the clear plastic wall
drawn and reaching, relentlessly,
like an insect, desperate against window glass,
seeing the other side so clearly
and wanting it so badly
unable to comprehend
this invisible barrier
separating us.

Other Mother

I am at her bedside
all day long.
My eyes see every little twitch
of her body and
every subtle hue of skin color;
no little flicker of change,
for better or worse,
escapes my attention,
and I respond,
immediately and intuitively,
my hands sure and steady,
my entire being
focused on her tiny frail body.

I stand over her,
sweating under hot bright lights,
my legs aching
from hours of standing,
my head throbbing
from concentration.
I don't feel my stomach
growling for lunch
and my bladder ready to burst
I don't feel a thing
except this commitment,
this passion, this sacred trust
placed in me,
and I won't leave her side
until I know that she is stable.

You cannot imagine
the details I know about her,
(what her blood gases have been
for the past twenty-four hours
how much urine she puts out every hour
the patterns of the tiny lines on her feet
the sound of air entering her lungs
how big her liver is).

But most important of all,
I know that you are her mother
and I am her nurse;
I promise you
that I know the difference
and so does she.
She needs us both, me for the present
and you forever.

But now, I am here, her nurse,
protective, powerful and determined, ready to do
Whatever it takes.

This is what we mean
by intensive care.

Questions

How can it be that a baby can die?
A baby's death is unfair, unnatural;
A baby's death upsets the balance, disturbs the order
throws the way of the world into reverse:
spring becomes winter
morning becomes night
a flower returns to the earth.
How can this be?

What do you call a parent whose baby dies?
If you lose your husband you're a widow;
lose your parents, you're an orphan.
Lose your baby? You're nothing.
There is no word because there is no way
to take all that pain and tie it up
in a neat package with a label.
What would you call it?

To whom do you pray, when a baby has died?
Do you pray to the God who took her away?
Who would give such a gift for such a short time?
What sort of God would play such a game
of giving and taking?
Taking a heart and breaking it
Taking a spirit and crushing it.
Take THIS, God—
Take this rage,
burning hotter than any fires of hell
Take this mother's screams and let them echo
forever in Your ears
Take this father's pain, his anguish,
His aching emptiness
if You must have this baby, too.
How do you pray?

How do you watch a baby die?
A tiny heart slows and finally rests.
Rosebud lips part and turn white.
Dancing arms and legs still and stiffen.
Warm, soft skin turns to yellow-white marble,
smooth and cold.
How do you watch? How do you wait?
How do you ever get through this?

How do you nurse a dying baby?
When it hurts so much
to see pain you'll never ease
Tears you'll never stop
and wounds you'll never heal.

How can you help?
Giving what comfort you can,
knowing there really is none
taking what comfort you can,
knowing that at least
you were there.
That you stayed to keep watch
and you stayed to keep warm
and you tried to keep safe.
And you say, "Little one, I am right here.
I'm staying with you. Please stay with me."
How can this be? Dear God, how can this be?

Soft Spots

An irresistible force
draws my hand
to stroke the little globe
of a newborn's head,
to feel its silken warmth
and the surprise
of the soft little dent,
the reminder that
a baby is unfinished
and so vulnerable.
Fontanelle, "little fountain,"
means source.
It is the spot
where you can touch
both fragility and strength.

Parents too have soft spots,
unfinished places
deep in their hearts
with no protection.
A wound inflicted there
may never heal
but this most tender place
is also a source
where you can find
both fragility and strength.

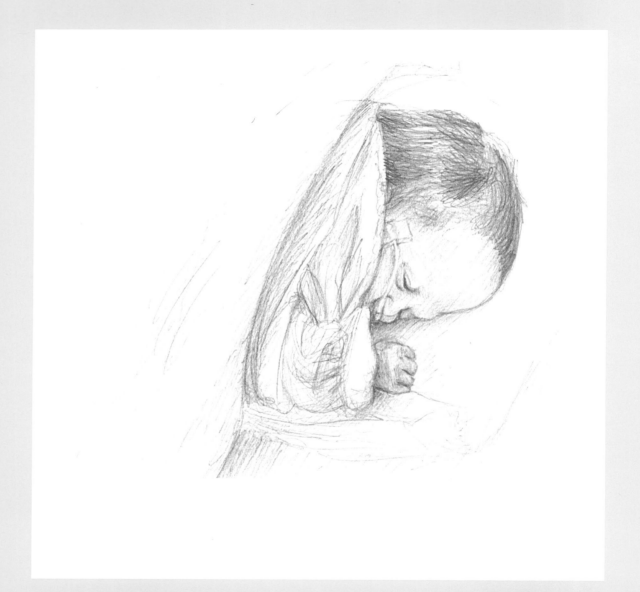

Adoption

Baby John
    sleeps in his Isolette®
all cozy warm contentment;
he's oblivious to the great big man
who towers over him,
white-haired and wrinkled
and wearing an uncertain frown.

With rough hands
big as baseball mitts
he holds on to the bed
and stands, staring for a long time
with worried eyes
at the tiny black-haired baby inside.

Slowly a smile creases his face and
he reaches in to touch
the smallest hand he's ever seen.
In a soft voice he whispers
"Hello grandson. Welcome to our family."

Premie Ballerina

She brings her hands together ever so slowly.
Her fingertips, barely touching, form a bridge
or a silent prayer.

She holds the pose and sits, unmoving,
like a dowager holding court,
plump pink face propped on a series of chins.

Her face is placid
only her deep blue eyes move, side to side
tracking the scene before her.

She sighs, seeming to approve,
then puckers her lips into a rosy pink "O"
as if expecting a kiss.

Gracefully she lifts one hand
and cradles her face, palm against cheek.
The other hand, abandoned, lingers briefly in mid-air;
her fingers flutter, then come to rest
lightly against her chest.

She takes a breath, then a deep yawn;
satisfied, she lowers her lids
and rests, in repose.

Prisoner of the Nursery

Baby boy with BPD
hooked up to oximetry
sleeping in your crib so sweet
wearing Bandaids® on both feet.

All big eyes and cherub cheeks
you barely grow from week to week;
your small body, always tired,
sporting all those tubes and wires;
Breathing fast and breathing hard,
never letting down your guard,
thrilling us with fleeting smiles
feeling good once in a while.

Baby boy with BPD
full of personality,
noble spirit, knowing eyes,
much too young to be so wise.
Is there someone you can trust
who understands what makes you fuss?
Is there anyone who sees
the fear you feel when your disease
takes your breath and makes you frantic
flailing, gasping, blue with panic?
Scrub suits soon surround your bed
to look at you and shake their heads.

Baby boy with BPD
Prisoner of the nursery.

Grandmother

She is so tired.
In the twilight of her life,
hair gone white against cinnamon skin,
she expected, finally, a chance to rest.
Her body is weary,
stiff and sore from all the years
of work — hard work, women's work —
raising babies, keeping house,
part time job in the hospital laundry,
always on her feet.

Now she is ready to sit.
She wants to watch TV, go to church,
have lunch with her lady friends
and drink her coffee slowly.
She looked forward
to the grandbabies
who would come over
to her neat quiet house
on Sunday afternoons.

Instead, her house is filled with kids and noise
and she is always on her feet, again,
raising the children of her children.
Relative custody is what
the judge called it
but she calls it unfair.

Late at night
she gets her chance to sit,
baby in her arms
and questions in her heart.
She is a quiet hero, everyday,
gracing her beautiful babies
with her soft smile and lilting voice
and seeing in their smooth round faces
traces of her own.

For them she is a source of strength and spirit;
she is both hope and history;
within her generous, giving body
she contains their past and their future.
She is a matriarch and a madonna
she is their grandmother.

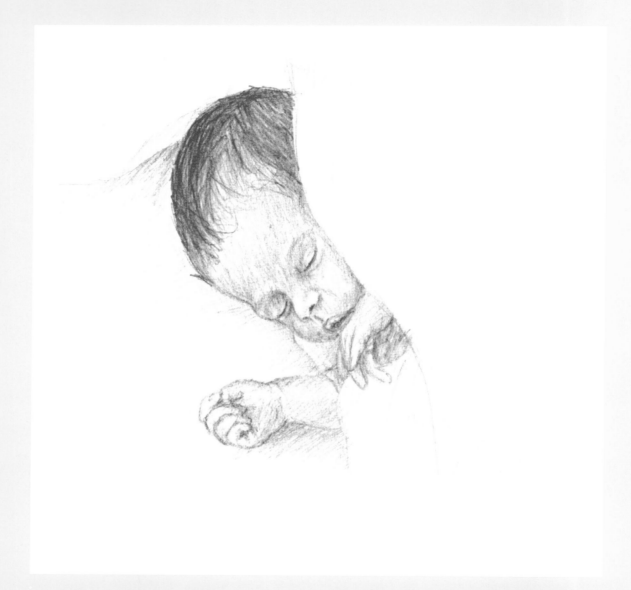

Allie Eight Weeks Old

Allie's hand is like a little flower;
fisted, a soft closed bud
that holds the promise of what
she will become.

Open, a pink and white rose,
lovely in full bloom
reaching out to touch
sunshine, sky and moon.

Dewy soft and smelling sweet
baby hands and baby feet.

Asphyxia

When birth and death coincide
all you get are vacant eyes
empty eyes that roll and stare
no questioning and no despair.

The first breath never taken
limbs stiff and tight with indignation
perfect bodies dead inside
little birds who cannot fly.

Who's to answer? Who's to blame?
When birth and death are all the same.

Vanessa

The mother's reputation arrived first.
  "No one has ever heard her speak."
"We think she may be retarded."
My first impression of Vanessa.

Assigned to be her nurse,
I took her on reluctantly, even angrily,
expecting failure.
I saw another hopeless, hapless scrap
for the social dump.
There we were, a pathetic trinity —
a premature child of a premature mother,
paired with this tired and cynical nurse.

She named the baby Julia,
a courageous and unusual choice in her world
and my first clue
that there was much more to Vanessa.
It took her three days
to make eye contact with me.
By that time I was enchanted
with her soft, slow ways, her gentle smile,
the way she remembered my suggestions.
She did everything I asked of her
and asked nothing of me.
She never spoke, but she never had to be told twice.
That was her way,
this little girl born last in a family of fourteen;
barely an afterthought,
she could hardly tolerate attention,
it was so foreign to her.

I told her that her name was beautiful,
a name for a princess.
We looked it up in the baby name book
and she glowed as I read it to her —
"Vanessa — a Greek word meaning butterfly."

She never uttered a word
but she smiled when I praised her
and nodded her head when she understood.
She did not shy away from my affection,
my hugs or my arm across her thin shoulders.

When discharge day finally came
Vanessa arrived alone, as always;
no one had ever visited with her.
Not even her own mother
had celebrated Julia's birth
or Vanessa's passage into motherhood.
As I walked her to the door
She turned to me, finally speaking and said,
"Thank you, Miss Nancy."
Thank you Vanessa, my little friend, my teacher.

Baby Holder

My hand cradles the silken globe
of the baby's head.
His warm weight satisfies my arms.

On my shoulder I sniff his fragrant cheek
and feel soft puffs of feathery breath
on my neck.

His hand grasps my finger
with surprising strength
and the small, steady breathing of his sleep
is a mantra that brings
peace to both of us.

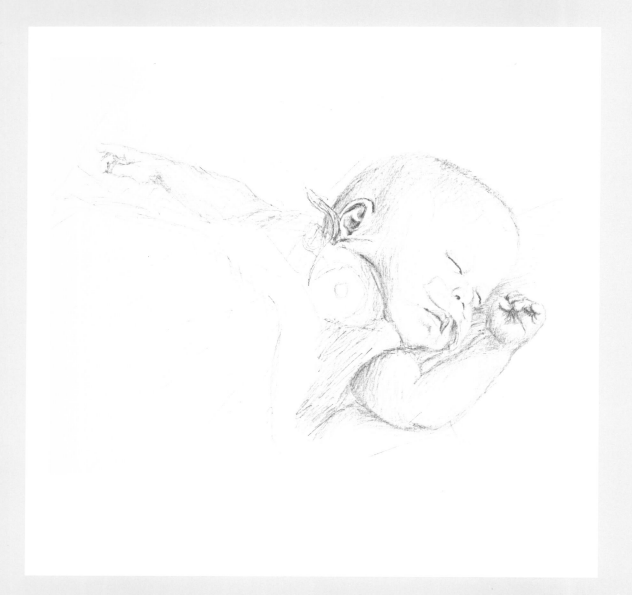

Zaire

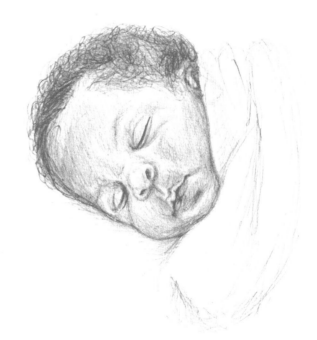

Soft fuzzy hair, rosebud lips,
brown soulful eyes and square fingertips.
Fat little feet, Michelin limbs,
dinner roll toes and multiple chins.
Long spiky lashes, satiny skin,
Kiss-me cheeks and sudden grin.

33

Baby Doctor (for Nilima)

I once heard her say
that a baby is the best thing
that can ever happen to you.
She believes that.

You can see it
in her warm healing hands and
in the slow smile she gives
to nervous parents.

She still feels it all, after many years
and her tears come as easily as her smile.

Pieta, Neonatal ICU

At home her arms ache
from nothing to hold,
a phantom pain
that she tries to relieve,
filling the emptiness with any warm bundle —
a sleepy cat, towels fresh from the dryer —
her need to hold
much deeper than her need to be held.

When she visits
the baby is placed in her arms
as she sits
in an old worn rocker;
she cradles him,
wrapped in the folds of her gown,
her head bent to gaze
into his closed peaceful face.

From the blankets encircling him,
a profusion of tubes emerge
and lay draped across her lap;
lifelines, but also tethers,
claiming possession,
always ready to snatch him back.

It comes down to this,
to these two,
mother and child forming
an island of stillness
in the center of a storm,
detached from the blurry motion
and noise of people
rushing around too importantly
to notice this tableau in their midst.

She sits in silence
and fights her fear alone
not always knowing
what to pray for anymore
and trusting only this:
that she is his mother,
his link with life
and the one constant
in the disarray of senseless events
that compose his life.

They take their cues
and their courage
from each other;
between them flows
a wordless communication,
a mutual sustenance,
and this,
the endless mother love,
a great tide flowing from her,
love at once both tender and fierce,
the love of all mothers
and all time and place,
this — ancient, eternal, universal force —
this is what shall heal them both.

Big Brother

He of the laughing eyes
and thoughtful frown
dances through the days
on limber little legs,
happy to be here,
happy to be himself.

He sprinkles his joy-dust
wherever he goes
leaving smiles in his wake
and lighting the world
with his radiance.

He is a prism
sparkling in the sun
giving off light in every direction
this powerhouse of a little person
four years old
and fabulous.

Amanda

The baby girl had no legs.
    Perfect feet jutted out sideways from her hips,
soft little feet
ten toes and ten fingers
being no guarantee of anything.
A gaping hole broke her face
where a nose and mouth should have been.
A hole in her throat gave her breath,
keeping her alive but depriving her of voice,
so that when she cried,
there was only silent thrashing;
there was no satisfaction in it.

But she made her presence known
and knew what she wanted;
she liked her father's strong solid arms
and the warm bubblebath that her mother
drove two hours a day to give her.
She had a pink bow taped to the side of her head
and she had a name.
She was Amanda,
and she insisted on herself.

Good Bye

Goodbye, good luck, and God bless you.
You're finally taking him home.
He's all dressed to go, in his car seat,
little prince sound asleep on his throne.

Do you know how to protect him?
Did you learn everything that we taught?
Do you have any more questions?
Is there anything that we forgot?

Tell us he'll never go hungry;
Promise you'll answer his cries.
Please do your best to be gentle,
You are the whole world in his eyes.

Remember that he's just a baby
Remember how little he is.
Hold him and love him and tell him he's good;
He is all yours and you are all his.

Goodbye, good luck, and God bless you
Have a life that is happy and free.
We hope that you, too, grow and blossom,
little mother, just barely fifteen.

Discharge

I knew you so well
little baby who will never know me.

Maybe you'll remember warm familiar hands
or the calm voice that coached you
through procedures and whispered
quiet comforts.

Maybe you sensed my eyes,
always watching, witnessing your growth,
or felt my presence
and trusted it somehow.

Maybe you felt my love.
Maybe you will remember.

Nancy Kennedy has been a neo-natal nurse for twenty years, working in various settings as a staff nurse, nurse educator, and manager. She is a graduate of St. Louis University. Nancy is currently the Clinical Administrator of Transitional Infant Care, a specialty hospital for high-risk infants that is part of The Children's Home of Pittsburgh.

David Pegher is an artist and teacher who graduated from Carnegie Mellon University in 1994. Dave became affiliated with Transitional Infant Care as a volunteer and soon began to sketch the infants. He was given the honorary title of Artist-in-Residence in recognition of his work. Dave has won local acclaim for his sensitive portraits and has had two exhibits at Pittsburgh galleries.